How to Design Functional level strategy

Hiriyappa. B, Ph.D.

Contents

Chapter 1. Marketing Strategy Formulation
Chapter 2. Financial Strategy Formulation
Chapter 3 Production Strategy Formulation
Chapter 4. Logistics Strategy
Chapter 5. Human Resource Strategy

CHAPTER 1

MARKETING STRATEGY FORMULATION

"As market windows open and close more quickly, it is important that R & D be tied more closely to corporate strategy".
William Spender

"Most of the time, strategists should not be formulating strategy at all; they should be getting on with implementing strategies they already have".
Henry - Mintzberg

INTRODUCTION

For effective strategy formulation, strategists have to provide valuable direction to functional managers regarding the plans and policies which are adopted by firms.

Functional strategies are typically: marketing, financial, production and human resources.

Functional strategies are based on the functional capability factors in firms.

For each functional area, we have to find the main areas and then discuss the sub areas of each functional area. These are regarding the content of functional strategies, important factors and the importance in the process of strategy formulation.

Functional strategies are operated below the strategic business units or business level strategies for functional level strategy formulation.

Functional level strategies consist of guidelines that are set at higher levels.

Functional managers need guidance and directions from the business strategy in order to make decisions which are related to the functional areas.

Operational plans explain the functional managers what has to be done meanwhile policies are stated how the plans are to be implemented.

REASONS FOR FUNCTIONAL STRATEGIES ARE NEEDED TO FIRMS

The development of functional strategies is formulated by the top-level management of the firm's. The functional level involves the execution of policy which made by the top level management. Strategic managers need to be segregated into viable functional plans and policies and avoid non-viable functional plans and polices which are compatible with each other in business. In this way, strategic managers in functional areas have discharged their role relating to functions in business. Strategic managers have studied of environmental factors which are affected by and relevant to firms. Organization strategies which have affected the choice of functional strategies. Finally, the actual process of choice is influenced by objectives as well as subjective factors in different functions. Major reasons for functional strategies are needed for firms are listed below:

The strategic decisions are implemented by all parts of a firm's/ organization.
There is a standard basis available for controlling activities in the different functional areas of the business.
When plans are clearly laid down that time functional manager to take decisions in flexible and short time and what is to be done

and executed policies provide the discretionary framework within which decisions are needed to be taken by functional managers in each function of the business.

Routine and similar situations are happened in different functional areas that are handled in a consistent manner by the functional managers in business.

Each functional manager in business should be taken coordination; it must take place in different functional areas in business.

MARKETING STRATEGY FORMUALATION

Marketing strategy formulation is one of the major tasks to business firms. Ordinary marketing strategy formulation is not a risk factor for firms; it is not created valuable impact to firms. Therefore, the present scenario, marketing strategy formulation that is considered to be the activities which are related to identifying the needs of customers and taking such actions which are satisfying them in the form of return of some consideration from a business. In marketing, it is more important to do what is right to do and what is immediately profitable venture to business to firms.

Relationship with marketing and other functions in business can be understood by the following mentioned factors:

Single marketing department cannot produce superior value for the customer. All company departments must work together to accomplish and satisfy customer needs and requirements.

Each department is a link in the value chain of firms.

A company's value chain is only as strong as the weakest link to firms.

Marketers are challenged to find ways to get all departments to think customers and search knowledge about customers.

Marketing competitive advantage and value chain gains should be taken purpose keep well partnering will produce a value delivery network; it consists of suppliers, distributors and ultimately customers. The value delivery network ensures that delivery of superior quality of services and products to the clients

Marketing Issues

Marketing issues relate to policies in market analysis, business law, display, salesmanship and advertising etc, i.e. they are concerned with total process of marketing which covering both product mix and market mix. The product mix includes decisions regarding the type, quantity and quality of product design, contents shape, methods and techniques of production etc. Market mix covers the issues like price, place, promotion, channels of distribution, advertising policies, packaging and branding decisions, consumer psychology and behavior and pricing of the product etc.

Since the modern concept of the market has treated as consumer as a king, every product is brought to satisfy customer needs. Hence its gamut is very fast. The policies in this field, therefore, deal with the following issues:

Organization's products / services; product life cycle and marketing strategy.

Concentration of sales in few products or little customer segmentation. Ability to gathered information about the market.

To know the market share or sub market share.

Product/service mix and expansion potential: to know the life cycle of key products; to know the profit or loss of the product/service.

To clearly know the channel of distribution; number, coverage, and control.

To maintain an effective sales organization: to find out knowledge about the customer needs.

To improve product/service quality with image and reputation of the brand name.

Efficient and effective utilization of available resource for effective sales promotion and advertising.

Too aware of the pricing strategy and pricing flexibility.

To effective monitoring and feedback on the marketing functions and expansion of production.

Effective implementation of after sales service and follow up. To keep standards, goodwill and brand loyalty.

Spotting out of the present and potential markets, the size and nature of consumers

The degree of competition in the market and how best could it be met. The location of prospects and persuading them to purchase.

Marketing Process

In company, once the strategic plan has been defined the company's overall mission and objectives, marketing plays a role in carrying out these objectives.

The marketing process is the process/stages of analyzing market opportunities, selecting target markets, development the market mix, and managing the marketing effort in business.

Target customers are standing in the Center of the marketing process in business.

Market is Connecting Customers

Today's market scenario is the competitive marketplace. Therefore, companies must be customer oriented towards the products and services. Companies must win customers and win competitors and keep them by delivering greater value goods and services. Since companies have to failure to satisfy all customer requirements and needs in the market. Companies must divide the total market on the basis segmentation and choose the best segments like market targeting and design strategies for profit oriented serving chosen segments and provide better services than their customers in the market.

Developing the Marketing Mix

Marketing mix is the combination of 4 P's i.e. product, price, place and promotion. The Company is decided to overall its competitive strategy. Firm's ready to begin planning the details of the marketing mix. The marketing mix is the set of controllable marketing variables in firm. Firms are using 4 P's and to produce valuable products and services and delivery to the ultimate users of the product and services. The marketing mix is consisting of everything that the firm ready to do and influence the demands for products and services from the customers.

Product

Product stands for the goods and service combination which offered by the company to the target market.

Strategies are required for adding new products and removing the failure products from markets.

Strategic decisions are related to the branding, packaging, and other product features like guarantee and warranty.

Price
Price refers to the amount of money which is paid by customers for obtaining the product and services from the company.

Pricing strategies are pertaining to the location of the customers, price flexibility, related items within a product line and terms of sale.

Pricing strategies are useful to companies for entering into the market especially with a new product that designed by the company.

Place
Place refers to the company activities that make the product and services are available to target consumers.

Strategist should be taken into the responsibility for distribution of goods and services to ultimate customers. In many cases, the ownership is transferred from company to customers.

Strategies applicable to middlemen like wholesalers, retails, must be designed by the company.

Promotion

Promotion refers to the activities that communicate the merits of the product and persuade target consumers to buy it from the company.

Strategies are needed to combine individual methods like advertising, personnel selling, and sales promotion into a coordinated campaign.

Promotional strategies must be adjusted as a product move from an earlier stage from the latest stage of its life.

For effective marketing program design purpose, blends all the marketing mix it elements into a coordinated program that in way to achieve the company's marketing objectives by delivering value to consumers in business.

The 4 P's seems to take the consumers and sellers view rather than the buyer's view and perhaps a better classification can be the 4 C's as outlined:

Product = Customer Solution
Price = Customer Cost
Place = Convenience
Promotion = Communication

Expanded Marketing Mix

Traditional mix is consisting of only 4 P's. Expanded marketing mix includes 4 P's plus people, physical evidence and process.

People

People refer to all human actors who have played a part in the delivery of the market offering by company and thus influence the buyer's perception, namely the firm's personnel and the customer in business.

Physical Evidence

Physical evidence refers to the environment in which the market offering goods, it is delivered by the company and where the firm and customer interact.

Process

Process refers to the actual procedures, mechanisms and flow of activities by which the product or services are delivered to client/customers.

Marketing Analysis

Marketing analysis generally involves a complete analysis of the company situation.

The company performs what its analysis

Clearly identifying environmental opportunities and threats.

Clearly analyzing company strengths and weaknesses to determine which opportunities the company can be pursued the best.

Get feed information and other outputs to each of the other marketing management functions in the company.

Marketing Planning

Generally marketing planning involves deciding on marketing strategies in the company. It will help to the company which attains its overall strategic objectives. A detailed and well-structured plan is needed for each business, product or brand. Particularly, a brand or product plan may contain different sections; executive summary, the current marketing situation, threats and opportunity analysis, objectives and issues, marketing strategies, action programs, budgets and controls.

Executive summary refers to a short summary of the main goals and recommendations to be presented in the marketing plan.

The current market situations refer to the section of a marketing plan that explains the target market and the company's position in it, important sections are outlined:

A market description
A product review
Analysis of the competition
A section on distribution.

In the threats and opportunities section refers to the managers forced to anticipate important developments that can have an impact on business either positive or negative to the firm.

Having studied the product's threats and opportunities refers to the managers can set objectives and consider issues that will affect them. The objectives should clearly state as goals that the company would like to attain during the plan's term in business operation.

Marketing strategy refers to the marketing logic by which the business unit hopes

To achieve its marketing objectives. Strategies should be created for all marketing mix components in business operation.

The market budget refers to the section of the marketing plan of company. It shows and projected revenues, costs, and profits of a firm.

Control is the last section of marketing plan; it refers to use to monitor progress. It allows for progress checks and corrective action of a firm.

Dealing with the Marketing Environment

A company must carefully analyze its environmental factors and in order to avoid the threats from the external environment and take advantage of the opportunities. Environmental areas to be analyzed as listed below:

Environment forces are to close the company like ability to serve customers, other company departments, channel members, suppliers, competitors and publics.

Environmental broader forces like demographic and economic forces, political and legal forces, technological and ecological forces and social and cultural forces.

MARKETING STRATEGY TECHNIQUES
Social Marketing

It refers to the design, implementation and control of programs. These are seeking to increase the acceptability in terms of a social ideas, cause or practice among a target group. For example, the publicity campaign for the prohibition of smoking in Bangalore explained the place where one can and can"t smoke in Bangalore.

Augmented Marketing

It refers to additional customer services and benefits built around the care and actual products which relate to introduction of high tech services such as movies on demand, online computer repair , services , secretarial services etc.,

These innovative offerings provide a set of benefits which promise to elevate customer services to unprecedented levels.

Direct Marketing

It refers to marketing through various advertising media which interact directly with customers.

It generally involves calling for the consumers to make direct response.

Direct marketing includes catalogue selling, mail, tele computing, electronic marketing, shopping and TV shopping.

It refers to the process of creating, maintaining, and enhancing strong, value based relationships with customers and stake holders.

It is very important to company to provide special e-services like services after a sale of the products and services.

It aims to provide to special benefits to customers to get new and existing customers in market.

Service marketing

Service marketing is applying the concepts, tools, and techniques for marketing to services.

Services are activity or benefit that one party can offer to another.

Services are the intangible.

Services do not result in the, banking, savings, retailing, educational or utilities.

Person Marketing

Person marketing refers to persons are marketing in the market.

Person marketing consists of activities that are undertaken to create, maintain or change attitudes or behavior towards particular people.

Example, politicians, sports stars, film stars, professional i.e., market themselves to get votes, or to promote their careers and earn income.

Organizing Marketing

It refers to activities which are undertaken to create, maintain, or change attitudes and behavior which relating to the target audience towards an organization.

Organizing market practice by profit and nonprofit organizations.

Place Marketing

It generally involves activities undertaken to create, maintain or change attitudes and behavior towards particular place.

Tourism marketing is the best example of place marketing.

Enlightened Marketing

It refers to marketing philosophy holding by the company that marketing should be supported to the best long run performance of the marketing system.

It consists of five principles are; customer oriented, marketing, innovative marketing, value marketing, senses of mission marketing and social marketing.

Differential marketing

Differential marketing refers to market coverage strategy in which a company can decide to target several market segments and make designs for separate offer each segment in market.

For instance, we shall take Hindustan Lever Limited has Lifebuoy, Lux and Rexona in popular segments and Liril and Pears in premium segments.

Synchromarkting

It refers to the demand for the product which is irregular due to season, some parts of the day, or an hourly basis, that can be causing idle capacity or over worked capacities.

Synchromarketing can be used to find ways to after the same pattern of demand through flexible pricing, promotion, and other incentives.

For instance, woolens or coolers; or hospitals undercooked on weekend or end of the week

Concentrated marketing
It refers to a market coverage strategy in which a company goes after a larger share of one or few sub markets.

Demarketing
It refers to marketing strategies is to reduce demand temporarily or permanently.

The aim is not to destroy demand, it only reduce demand or shift it.

These things are happening when overfull demand.

For example, buses are overloaded in the morning and evening, at the same time roads are busy for most of the times, Zoological parks are overcrowded on Saturdays, Sundays and holidays.

It can be applied to regulate demand.

CHAPTER 2

FINANCIAL STRATEGY FORMULATION

INTRODUCTION

The financial management strategies are related to several finance and accounting functions in organization. Finance and accounting concepts are to be considered as central for strategy implementation. Financial information are; acquiring, needed capital, sources of fund, developing projected financial statements, budgets, management, usage of funds and evaluating the worth of business, ratio analysis, cash flow statement, maintain of books of accounts etc. strategist need to formulate financial strategies relating above mentioned issues in finance areas for implementation in organization.

FINANCE AND ACCOUNTING POLICIES

Finance and accounting policies are outlined:

Ability to raise short term and long-term capital: either debt or equity.

To maintain good corporate level resource.

To know the cost of capital relative to industry and competitors

Tax consideration

To build up effective relationships with owners, investors, financial institution and stock holders.

To know the leverage position: capacity to utilization financial strategies, like lease or sale and lease back.

To aware of the cost of entry and barriers of the entry.

To know the price earnings ratio

Present working capital position of the organization.

Effective cost control and the ability to minimize the cost of expenditure for the production of goods and service.
Financial size of the organization.

Efficient and effective accounting system for cost, budget, and profit planning of the organization.

To determine liquid position in the organization and determine the cash flow and fund flows and ratio analysis in organization.

Account receivables and account payables, cost center, types of cost and standard and actual cost performance in organization.

ACQUIRING CAPITAL TO IMPLEMENT STRATEGIES / SOURCES OF FUNDS

Successful strategy implementation often requires and brings additional capital to business organization

Organization capital acquiring is based on the two important components such as equity and debt

Capital structure is the combination of debt and equity; it is very vital to company for successful of business operations in this way maximize the benefits to the company.

Companies have enough debt in its capital structure to boost its return on investment by applying debt to products and projects earning more than the cost of the debt.

In low earning periods, too much debt in capital structure components of an organization can endanger to stock holders return and jeopardize to organization survival.

Fixed debt is very important to company to keep its financial status in constant manner and avoid to overpaying to debt holders due to pay fixed percentage of return to the debt holder in business.

If company is earning more profit, this company collects too much debt from public and reduces equity ratios in capital structure. It is more impact to business to maximize the benefits to business operations.

Mergers, takeovers, acquisitions are the serious issues in today's scenario in acquiring capital.

Major Factors Regarding In Financial Strategy

Capital structure

Procurement of capital and working capital borrowings

Reserves and surplus as source of funds relating with lenders, banking and financial institutions

Source of funds is the important for implantation of the financial strategies in organization.

Organizations having the different range of source of funds alternatives in the form that a company may rely on external borrowing and another company can be followed the internal policy of finance

Projected Financial Statements / Budget

Projected financial statement analysis is a central strategy implementation technique.

It allows an enterprise to examine the expected results of various actions and approaches relating the finance and accounting.

This analysis is used for estimation of future and impact of various implementation decisions in organization.

Financial institutions request the projected financial statement when an organization seeks capital from the financial institutions.

For this, an enterprise should prepare ratio analysis, fund flow statement and financial statements which are computed projected financial ratios under various strategy implementation scenarios.

Financial statements and ratio have been providing the insight feasibility of company or enterprise for past years and current years for various strategy implementation approaches.

Projected Financial Budget

Financial budget is the statement of income and expenditure for the particular period.

It is documented which provides details how funds will be obtained and spent for a specified period of time.

Annual budget is most common. Budget period ranges from one day to more than ten years. It is depending upon the firm's decisions.

Financial budget will specify the needs and requirement for implementation of financial budget in a company.

It is not a tool for limiting expenditure but rather as a method for obtaining the most productive and profitable use of an organization core resources.

It can be viewed as the planned allocation of firm resources which are based on forecasts of the future.

Types of budget

Common types of budget are listed below:

Cash budgets

Operating budgets

Sales budgets

Profit budgets

Factory budgets

Capital budgets

Expenses budgets

Variable budgets

Flexible budgets

And fixed budget

When an organization is facing problems for this purpose a strategist use budget which are especially important in guiding strategy implementation.

Limitations of Financial Budget

Budgets are expensive and cumbersome to the company

Over budget and under budget can be caused problems to the company

Financial budget is the subjective for objectives

It is a tool and not an end in itself

The real budget can be hidden inefficiencies if it is based on solely precedents rather than on periodic evaluation of the circumstances and standards.

Budgets are sometimes used as instruments of tyranny i.e domination that result is frustration, resentment, absenteeism and higher turnover.

To minimize the effect of budget, it is last concern, when managers should increase the participation of subordinates in preparing budgets

Management / Usage of Funds

Management or usage of funds refers to the investment of funds or asset mix decisions.

Plans and policy are to be made by the company, plans and policies are listed below:

Capital investment

Fixed assets acquisitions

Current assets

Loans and advances

Dividend decisions

Relationship with shareholders.

Management of funds related to the efficiency and effectiveness of scarce resource utilization in firms in the process of strategy implementation.

Result of Implementations of Usage of Project

Implementation strategy is the results in increase in capital work in progress and current assets.

It plans and policy is not clear, the usage of funds is inefficient which will be leading to less than an optimum utilization of core resources

It is also considered by firms to attract and retain shareholders interest in market.

Dividend policy and bonus distribution policy is very important to usage funds in projects.

Management of funds

Management of funds is also an important area of financial strategies in firms.

Management of funds basically refers to the decisions which are to the systemic aspects of financial management.

The major policies and funds relating in business enterprise deals with the following issues:

The systems of finance

The systems of accounting

The systems of budgeting

The systems of managerial controlling

The systems of cash and credit

The systems of risk **management**

The systems of cost control and reduction

The system of tax planning and advantages

Effective management of funds can be played a pivotal role in strategy formulation, it is to be aimed to achieve by the company by optimum utilization of funds objectives, these are playing a central role for strategic action in the company.

Grand strategies like expansion, growth, retrenchment cannot escape from proper fund management in firms.

Good fund management and efficient strategy implement will be brought result to the company. Apart from the improper management of funds will be brought failure in strategy implementation in companies.

Strategist responsibilities is the minimizing the conflict of interest between the management and shareholders for effective utilization of funds, procurement of funds and allocation of funds.

EVALUATING THE WORTH OF A BUSINESS

Evaluating the worth of a business is the central and core role of the implementation strategy, it is integrative, intensive and diversification strategies are implemented and acquiring by the other firms in the market, Retrenchment strategy is the result of sale of division, portion of business in organization. Successful implementation strategies should be considered the financial worth or cash value of a business.

Different Approaches to be Determining the Worth of a Business.

Determining the worth of a business can be grouped into three main approaches in the enterprise.

First Approach

Evaluating the worth of a business which is determining its net worth or stock holder's equity.

Net worth of company represents the sum of common stock, additional paid capital and retains earnings.

After calculated the net worth, we shall do add or subtract an appropriate amount for goodwill and overvalued or undervalued assets.

It total value provides a reasonable estimate of a firm's monetary value.

In the case, the firm has goodwill; it will be listed on the balance sheet, although its intangible assets i.e. goodwill.

Second Approach
It is measuring the value of a firm grows out of the belief which is the worth of any business should be based on largely on the future benefits its owners may derive through net profits.

In another thumb of rule, it is to establish a business worth as five times the firm's current annual profit. For this purpose, we shall consider a five-year average profit level can also use.

When using this approach, the firm's normally surplus earnings and it shows in financial statements and minimize taxes to firms.

Third Approach

The net worth of a business is determined by market.

This approach involves three methods are listed below:

I. Firm's base worth on the selling price of similar company.
It deals with the potential problems in the forms of comparable figures are not available , not easy to locate, although the firm's has substantial information to buy or sell to other firms in the market.

II. The price earning method

This method divides the market price of the firm's common stock by the annual earnings per share and multiply this number by the firm's average net income for the past five years.

III. Outstanding shares method

This method involves the multiply the number shares outstanding by the market price per share and add a premium. The premium is simply a per share amount. A firm or person willing to pay a premium amount to control or acquire the other company.

CHAPTER 3

PRODUCTION STRATEGY FORMULATION

INTRODUCTION

The production strategies are relating to production system, operational planning and control, and research and development.

Production strategies are adopted which are affected to firm's nature of products or services, how these served to market, and the manner in which these strategies are served in markets.

All these influences to firm's production operations systems structure and objectives which are used to determine the operations plans and policies relating to the production.

The operation system structure is concerned with the manufacturing or service and supply or delivery system, and operations system objectives, these are related to customer services and resource utilization which are determined the operations, plans and policies are set in the firm's activities.

PRODUCTION/OPERATION/TECHNICAL ISSUES

Production or operation or technical issues are as follows:

To know the present raw material cost and availability

Inventory control system of the organization.

Location facilities; layout and utilization facilities.

Technical efficiency and effective utilization of technical resource in the organization.

Effective use and implementation of subcontracting.

Degree of vertical integration in terms of value added and profit margin of the product.

To know the efficient and cost benefit of production techniques.

Effective utilization and implementation of operation control procedure: design, scheduling, purchasing, quality control and efficiency.

To know the costs and technological competencies relative to industry and competitors.

Research development, innovative, advance ethnological development.

Patents, trademarks and similar legal protection for their organization products/service.

Production system
Production system is concerned with the capacity, location, layout, product or services design, work systems, degree of automation, extent of vertical integration.

Production strategies are significant and play vital issues which are affecting the capability of the organization goals and objectives for achievement of both.

Production strategy implementation is considered into account in the production system and used for decisions which are long term in nature. These are influence not the only operations capability of an organization. Apart from the ability to implement strategies and achieve strategic objective in the company.

Operations Planning and Control

Strategies are related to operations planning and control is concerned with aggregate production planning, materials supply, inventory cost and quality management and maintenance of plant and equipment in firm's level.

It is the aim of strategy implementation, for this purpose, we have to see how efficiently resources are utilized and in what manner the day to day operations can be managed in the light of long term objectives.

Operations planning and control provides to plan and control production process in the company.

It deals with the centralized the operations planning and decentralized the operation planning. It involves the testing, standardization and fabricating the equipment.

Few companies are uses the quality is the strategic tool. it helpful to design the test the quality inspection., standardization in terms of quality engineering.

CHAPTER 4

LOGISTICS STRATEGY

INTRODUCTION

Logistics strategy is one of the important strategy to management in formulate logistic strategy at the supplies of goods and services to customers.

It is process of integration of the flow of supplies of material by the organization to customers in this way achieve a level of services that ensures the right materials are available at the right place, at the right time, of the right quality and at the right cost.

It involves the transportation of goods and services from company to customer place as it is low as possible consistent with safe and reliable delivery.

Supply chain management helps with logistics and it enables to company to have constant contact with its distribution team that consists of trucks, trains, or any other mode of transportation.

Emerging Technological changes and industrial initiatives are helpful to logistic strategy for successful development of logistics strategy formulation of firm's.

Firms are effective logistic strategy will be involved for rising and finding major solutions to the following questions are outlined:

What are the sources of raw materials and components are available to firms?

How many manufacturing locations owned by firm's?

What are the products are produced or manufactured at each location?

What is the mode of transport for goods and services which manufactured by company?

What is the nature of distribution facilities of firms?

What is the nature of materials handling equipment possessed? What is ideal to firms?

What is the method for deploying inventory in the logistics network of firms?

Is any transport vehicles either owned by company or not?

IMPROVEMENT OF LOGISTICS

Effective strategy implementation results ensure that the following improvements for firms:

Cost saving to company

Reduced inventory system for company

Increased the customer satisfaction

To take competitive advantage

RESEARCH AND DEVELOPMENT STRATEGY

Research and development can play a significant role and integrated with part of strategy implementation.

It refers to the development of new products and improving the old products by adding new features to old products and services.

Effective research and development strategy implementation results ensure that the quality products, quality services, and reduced the cost of products and services, satisfying the customer needs and requirements.

Research and development department is one of the valuable department in firms, this department consists skillful resource persons who are performing tasks like transferring complex technology, adjusting processes to local raw materials, adapting process to local markets, and altering products to particular tastes and specifications.

Product development, market penetration and concentric diversification strategies are required to develop new products and services successfully developed and also significantly improved to old products into new version products for this purpose effective and excellence of research development is required to all types of business operations in market.

Technological developments are affected to company's products and services which are offered to the ultimate customers. It is affected by consumer and industrial products and services shorten product life cycles.

Technological advancement will be taken by the company in the form of increasing the profitability and enhance the customer base including existing and old and new customers in the market, able to reveal to rivalries in the market.

Majority of the survey shows that effective research and development strategy that ties external opportunities to enhance the internal strengths and these things linked with the objectives of firms.

WELL FORMULATED RESEARCH DEVELOPMENT STRATEGY RESULTS

Well formulated research development strategy results enhance the opportunities from internal and externally from the company environment. The major results are outlined:

It emphasis on product or process improvements

It is basic or applied research

To be leaders or followers in R&D

It develops to robotics or manual type processes

To perform R&D within the firm or to contract R&D to outside of firms.

To use universal researchers or private sector researchers.

There must be effective interactions between R&D department and other functional departments in implementing different types of generic business strategies like focus strategy, leadership strategy and grand strategy. Avoid and minimize the conflicts between marketing, finance or accounting, R&D and information systems departments and make clear policies and objectives of company.

PROPER GUIDELINES FOR RESEARCH AND DEVELOPMENT STRATEGIES

Proper guidelines for research and development strategies are listed below:

In the case, the company's technical progress slow , its result in market rate is moderate and significant barriers to possible new entrants, it can be clarified to company in house R& D is preferred for solution. In the case, research and development strategies are successful; it will result in a temporary products and process monopoly that can be exploiting by the company.

In the case, the technology change is rapidly and the market is growing slowly in this case the research and development involves very risk due to lead to new development of an ultimately obsolete technology or one for which there is no market for products and services which offered by company.

In the case, technology change is slow in spite of the market is growing quickly, in this case, there is not enough time for in house development. In this prescribed approach, it is to obtain R&D expertise on an exclusive or non exclusive basis from an outside firm.

In the case, both technical progress and market growth are very fast. These circumstances, R&D expertise should be obtained through acquisition of a well established firm in the industry.

RESEARCH AND DEVELOPMENT APPROACHES

There are three approaches for implementation of R&D strategies:

First Approach

Firm is to make technological products
This strategy approach is the glamorous and exciting and dangerous one to firms.

When competitor makes a technological product than only pioneer firms are fallen in marketing and rival firms seizing this initiatives.

Second Approach

Firm is to an innovative imitator of successful products.

It minimizing the risks and costs starts up in business.

This strategy approach entails and allowing a pioneer firm have to develop the first version of the new product and to introduce to existing market.
Excellent R& D personnel and Marketing department is the basic requirement for firms.

Third Approach
Firm is to be a low cost producer of mass producing products

This approach is less expensive and products are recently introduced by the firms.

A product prices is increased when a new product accepted by customers.

This approach requires substantial investment for buying of plant and equipment, in spite of fewer expenditure compare first and second approach in R&D.

Research, Technology and Systems Delivered

Research, technology and systems delivered are essential requirement of the company. Research, technology and systems delivered are as outlined.

Activities

Costs and assets relating to product R&D,

Process R&D

Process design improvements

Equipment design

Computer software development

Telecommunications system

Computer assisted designs and engineering

New data base capabilities

Development of computerized support systems.

The R&D function develops new product and its process technologies. Technological innovation result is lower manufacturing costs and result in the creation of more attractive products that demand a premium price. It can affect primary manufacturing and marketing activities, and through them value creation.

CHAPTER 5

HUMAN RESOURCE STRATEGY

INTRODUCTION

Human resources management refers to recruitment, hiring, training, development and compensation of the employees of the organization. Human resource management activities are as follows:

Activities Costs

Assets associated with the recruitment, hiring training, development, and compensation of all types of personnel.

Labor relations activities

Developed of knowledge based skills and core competencies.

The human resource function ensures that the company or organization has the right mix of skill people to perform its value creation activities effectively.

Human resource strategy plays significant role in implementation of strategy in company.

The job of human resource manager is changing rapidly as their companies that downsize and recognize employee's requirements for projects.

Strategic responsibilities of the human resource manager as listed below:

Assessing the staffing needs

And costs for of alternative strategies proposed during strategy formulation and developing in firms.

Staffing plan for effectively implementing strategies in firms. This plan must consider how best to manager calculated to the individual costs in firm.

The plan must also include how to motivate employees and manager's firms.

The human resource department must develop performance incentives that clearly link between the performance and pay to employees in this way to achieve human resource strategies.

It is process of empowering to implement human resource strategies;

it is responsibilities of managers and employees in firm and their involvement in strategic management activities that yields the greatest benefits when all organizational members can be understood clearly and to know how they will benefit personally if the firm does well.

It clearly linking between company duties and responsibilities and personal benefits is a major new strategic responsibility of human resource managers.

Other new responsibilities for human resource managers may include: establishing and administering an employee stock ownership plan (ESOP), instituting an effective childcare policy, and providing leadership for managers and employees in this way to allows them balance to with work and family.

HUMAN RESOURCE STRATEGIES PROBLEMS

Well-designed strategic management system can be failed if sufficient attention is not given to human resource dimension in firms.

Human resource problems arise when business implement strategies can usually have traced to three causes as listed below:

I. Disruption of social and political structures failure to match individual's aptitudes with implementation tasks III. Inadequate top management support for implementation activities

Human Strategy implementation poses a threat to many managers and employees in organization due to new power and status management relationships are anticipated and realized in firms. New formal and informal groups, values, beliefs, and priorities may be largely unknown by managers and employees, these things may become engaged in resistance behavior as their roles prerogatives and power in the firm change. Disruption of social and political structures that accompany with strategy execution, it must be anticipated and considered during strategy formulation and managed during strategy implementation process.

MAJOR TASKS OF HUMAN RESOURCE STRATEGY

Human resource strategies are concerning matching managers with strategy specify that jobs have specific and relatively static responsibilities, although people are dynamic in their personal development it is commonly used methods that will be matched managers with strategies to be implemented in firm's. it is including transferring managers task and duties for this purpose developing workshops, offering career development activities, promotions, job enlargements and job enrichment to employees of the firm's.

MAJOR GUIDELINES FOR HUMAN RESOURCE STRATEGY

A number of other guidelines can help to human resource managers and ensure that human relationship facilities in firms rather than disrupt strategy implementations efforts. Specifically, HR managers should do a form of chatting and informal questioning to stay abreast of how things are progressing and to know when to intervene to employees of the firm's. HR managers can be building proper support for strategy implementation. Mangers are put efforts by giving few order, announcing few decisions, depending heavily on informal questioning and seeking to probe and clarify until a consensus emerges with human resource in projects. It is one of the key thrusts that needed should be taken in the form of rewarded that generously and visibly in firms. It is surprising that so often during strategy formulation shall consider individual values, skills, and abilities needed for successful strategy implementation in firms. It is very rare that a firm selection new strategies which are significantly altering an existing strategies possesses by the firm's at the right line and staff personnel in the light positions, for successful strategy implementation. These things are needed to match individual aptitudes with relevant strategy implementation tasks should be considered with strategic choice.

Inadequate support from strategies for implementation activities often undermines organizational success. Apart from chief executive officers, small business owners, and government agency heads must be personally committed to strategy implementation and expenses commitment highly visible ways in enterprise. Strategist formal statements about the importance of strategic management, it must consistent switch with actual support and rewards given for activities completed and should be objectives reached. Otherwise, stress will be created by inconsistency, it can cause uncertainty among manages and employees at all levels in business enterprises.

Perhaps the best method for preventing and overcoming human resource problems in strategic management, it is to activity which involved by many managers and employees as possible in this process. Although, it is time consuming, this approach will be understanding, trust, commitment and ownership and reduces resentment and hostility. The true potential of strategy formulation and implementation presides by skilled and trained people in enterprise.

The firm's external opportunities and threats are on the one hand, and its internal strengths and weakness are on the other hand. In human resource strategic management, the competitive advantage may be in the form of low costs relationship in the industry or being unique in the industry along dimensions that are widely used by the customers in particular segments and society at large. And so that they can obtained a competitive edge by becoming a low cost leader or differentiator put heavy a premium on having highly competent and commitment team for human resources.

ACCORDING TO CHARLES GREER

"In a growing number organizations, human resource are now viewed as source of competitive advantage, there is greater advantage that distinctive competencies are obtained through highly developed employed skills, distinctive organizational cultures management processes and systems".

The role of human resource enabling an organization to effectively deal with the external environment challenges. The human resource management function has been accepted as a strategic partner in the formulation of organizations strategies, implementation of such strategies through human resource planning employment, training, appraisal, and compensation practices of employees, these are strongly influence on employees competence is very important to business enterprise.

Recruitment and selection; in this process, the workforce will be more competent if a firm can successfully identity, attracts, and select and most competent applicants on market.

Training: in this process, the workforce will be more competent if employees are well trained to perform their job property.

Appraisal of performance: it refers to the performance appraisal is to identify and performance deficiencies experienced due to lack of competences. Such deficiencies, once identified, can often be solving through counseling, coaching or training in business enterprise.

Compensation: it refers in a firm can usually increase the competency of its workforce by offering paid and benefit packages that are more attractive than those of their competitors, these proactive enables organizations to attract and retain the most capable people in jobs.

STRATEGY AND HUMAN RESOURCE MANAGEMENT

The human resource strategy of business should reflect and support the corporate strategy.

An effective human strategy includes the way in which the organization plans to develop its employees and provide them suitable opportunities and better working conditions so that their optional contribution is ensured. This implies selecting the best available personnel in this way to ensuring a fit between the employees and the job and retaining, motivating, and empowering employees to perform well in the direction of corporate objectives.

Strategic human resource management may be defined as **the linking of human**

resource management with strategic goals and objectives to improve business performance and develop organizational culture that fosters innovation and flexibility. The success of an organizational depends on its human resource. This refers to how they are acquired, developed, motivated and retained. Organizational play is an important role in organizational success. The pre supposes an integrated approach towards human resource functions and overall business functions of an organization.

The human resource management practice of an organization may be an important source of competitive advantage. For this strategic have focused should be given in the following points.

Pre selection practices including human resource planning and job analysis in business enterprise.

Selection practice refers to staff various positions in the organizations and predefined requirement and selection policies and procedures should be designed keeping in view the mission and the purpose of an organization.

Post selection practices is to maintain and improve the workers job performance levels, human resources decisions related to training and development, performance appraisal, compensation and motivation should be based on corporate strategy of the organization.

STRATEGIC ROLE OF HUMAN RESOURCE MANAGEMENT

The prominent areas where human resource manager can play strategic role are as follows:

Providing Purposeful Direction

The human resource management must be able to lead people and the organization towards the desired direction,

It is involving the right people for the right job from the beginning.

The most important tasks of professional management is to ensure that the object of an organization has been internalized by each individual working in the organization.

Goals of an organization state the clear purpose and justification of its existence in business enterprise.

Creating Competitive Atmosphere

Presents globalize market maintaining a competitive gain is the object of any organization.

There are two important ways of business can be achieved a competitive advantage over the others. The first is cost leadership which refers to the firm

aims to become a low cost leader in the industry. The second competitive strategy is differentiation under which the firm seeks to be unique in the industry in terms of dimensions that are highly valued by the customers.

Putting these strategies into implementations that effect carries a heavy premium on having a highly committed and competent workforce.

Facilitation of Change
The human resource will be more concerned with substance rather than form, accomplishments rather than activities, and practice rather than theory.

The personnel function will be responsible for furthering the organization not just maintaining it.

Human resource management will have to devote more time to promote changes than to mainatain the status quo in business operations.

diversion of workforce

In the modern organization management refers to diverse workforce is a great challenge.

Workforce diversity can be observed in terms of male and female workers. Young and old workers, educated and unrelated workers. Unskilled and professional employees ect,

Moreover, many organizations also have people of different castes, religious and nationalities.

The workforce in future will comprises more of educated and self conscious workers. They will ask for high people of degree of participation and avenues for fulfillment.

Money will no longer be the sole motivating force for the majority of the worker. Non financial incentives will also play an important role in motivating the workforce.

Empowerment of human resource;

Empowerment means authorizing every number of a society or organization to take of his/ her own destiny realizing his/ her full potential.

Empowerment means authorizing every number of a society or organization to take of his / her own destiny realizing his/ her full potential.

It involves to be given more power to those who, at present, have little control what they do and little ability to influence the decisions being made around them.

Building core competency;

The human resource manager has a great role to play in developing core competency by of the firm.

A core competency is a unique strength of an organization which may not be shared by others.

This may be in the form of human resource, marketing capacity, or technological capability.

If the business is organized on the basis of core competency, it is likely to generate competitive advantage. because of this reason, many organizations have restructuring their business around by divesting those business which do not match core competences implies leveraging and limited resources of a firm.

It needs creative courage's and dynamic leadership having faith in organization human resources.

organizations human resource.

development of works ethics and culture;

Greater efforts will be needed to achieve cohesiveness because workers will have transient commitment to groups.

As changing work ethic requires increasing emphasis on individuals, job will have to be redesigned to provide challenge.

Flexible starting and quitting times for employees may be necessary.

focus will shift form extrinsic to intrinsic motivation. A vibrant work culture will have to be developed in the organizations to create an atmosphere of trust among people and to encourage creative ideas by the people.

It is far reaching changes with the help of technical knowledge will be required for this purpose.

Human resource development functions are as outlined:

Effective management of the human resource in the organization. Improvement of employee skill and morale.

Labor relations costs compared to industry and competition from present industry scenario.

Efficient and effective formulation and implementation and controlling of the policies.

Effective utilization of incentive to motivate employees" performance. To know the ability to level peaks and valleys of employment.

To regulate employee turnover and absenteeism. Specialized skills and experience

www.ingramcontent.com/pod-product-compliance
Lightning Source LLC
Chambersburg PA
CBHW030502220526
45464CB00006B/2624